Beauty of
Washington, D.C.

Beauty of
Washington, D.C.

Text: William C. Curran
Concept & Design: Robert D. Shangle

First Printing August, 1992
Published by LTA Publishing Company
Division of Renaissance Publishing Company, Inc.
318 East 7th St., Auburn, IN 46706

"Learn about America in a beautiful way."

This book features the photography of
James Blank
Robert Shangle
Charlie Borland

Library of Congress Cataloging-in-Publication Data
Beauty of Washington, D.C.
/text, Curran, William, 1921-
    p.   cm.
ISBN 0-917630-73-4; $19.95 — ISBN 0-917630-72-6 (pbk.); $9.95
    Rev. ed. of: Beautiful Washington, DC., c1979.
    1. Washington (D.C.) — Description — 1981 — Views.
I. Shangle, Robert D.   II. Curran, William, 1921-   . III. Title.
F195.C88   1989
917.5304'4   89-35183

Copyright © 1992 by LTA Publishing Company
Division of Renaissance Publishing Company, Inc.
Printed in the United States of America

Contents

Introduction

Washington D.C. may be the model of national capitals. "It is the only large city in the world," wrote Washington sage Willard M. Kiplinger, "devoted exclusively to government, without the leavening of other normal human occupations." London is one of the world's largest banking centers and one of the world's greatest deep-water ports. Paris and Moscow are major centers of international trade and manufacture and lie on important navigable waterways. If any of these was suddenly to lose its governmental function, it would go right on playing a major role in the life of its nation and the world. Washington, on the other hand, except as headquarters for our Federal Government, is unimaginable.

When in 1790 Congress asked George Washington to select a site for the newly authorized federal capital "somewhere in the vicinity of the Potomac River" and "not exceeding ten-miles square," (i.e., ten miles on a side) the first President responded like the former soldier and surveyor that he was. He first did a careful and systematic reconnaissance of more than 90 miles up and down the river. Then he made his recommendation. There can be little doubt that he made the best choice. In the beauty of its natural surroundings and on its admirable accessibility, the area still works well as a national capital, even 200 years later. Nothing could have been more appropriate than Congress' naming the district for Washington.

The original grants of land from Maryland and Virginia provided the new District of Columbia with a generous hundred square miles in which to grow. By the 1840s, this seemed to be more than would ever be used and so the portion west of the river was receded to Virginia at her request. This reduced the District to its present 68-square miles, a sloping V-shaped plain between the Potomac on the west — a majestic one-mile wide at this point — and the short, but broad, Anacostia on the east.

Despite its somewhat swampy character, the site and terrain were ideally suited for the imperial capital envisioned by Pierre L'Enfant, the spirited former French military engineer appointed by Washington to help lay out the city. The Frenchman dreamed of a super-Paris or a Constantinople, a city of 400-foot-wide boulevards, of grand public monuments, vast plazas, magnificent distances, all set off by acres and acres of lavishly cultivated greenery. Before he could give form to his dream, L'Enfant ran afoul of the country's first real estate lobby. It didn't take a lot of figuring for the early land speculators to realize that the Frenchman's ambitious dimensions weren't leaving much of that hundred-square miles for their tenements. Their protest was loud and strong.

At first Washington stood firm and backed his city planner. In time, however, he fired the headstrong L'Enfant just to keep peace. Happily for the nation, before the Frenchman could be ordered to roll up his steel tape, he had managed to fix his indelible stamp on the face of the city. In the 1870s President Ulysses Grant directed Commissioner of Public Works, Alexander "Boss" Shepherd, to dust off L'Enfant's plan and finish the job as best he could. Shepherd did a whale of a job.

Although he did not live to see it, L'Enfant's plan was realized: not only his broad boulevards and grand vistas, but also the wealth of greenery he had dreamed of. Early on it must have been discovered that a startling variety of trees, shrubs, and flowers would thrive in the mild, moist climate of the Potomac basin, and many exotics were introduced into the city, often by Americans who had served abroad, or, later, by members of the large international community.

It's possible that Washington outdoes all other American cities in the amount of space given over to growing things. Officially, there are over 750 parks, totaling almost 8,000 acres, ranging from giant Rock Creek at just under 2,000 acres down to playgrounds for pre-schoolers. Add to these the campuses of six universities, the National Arboretum, the spacious grounds of institutions like St. Elizabeth's Hospital, Washington Cathedral, the Franciscan Monastery, and Walter Reed Medical Center and it's no surprise that when seen from the air in summer Washington appears as a green expanse punctuated by white buildings.

In reality Washington has several "faces" and it is possible to use architecture to identify different parts of the city. From the Library of

Congress to the Kennedy Center, and from Pennsylvania Avenue to the Potomac, the dominant structure is the massive stone building, usually incorporating some classical, renaissance, or medieval motives. North of Pennsylvania Avenue, roughly as far as Massachusetts Avenue, is "downtown," an area of white brick, concrete, steel, and glass — office buildings, stores, hotels, and restaurants. This is the city's central retail and financial district. Much of the remainder of the District is residential, and if it has a characteristic structure, it is the brick row houses, especially east of the Capitol and in Georgetown. Made from iron-rich local clay, the building bricks give the houses an unmistakable appearance. The larger houses — and this would be true in Georgetown — are sometimes classics of the Federal style. Even the small ones have a special charm and often feature bay windows, cast-iron fences around tiny yards, and brick walkways shaded by small ailanthus trees.

Like most cities, Washington has its mythology: the collection of stories long-time residents like to tell about "what it's really like" to live there. Stories of this nature tend to consist mainly of complaints, to be sure, but in order to survive, they have to be at least partly true. A quick rundown of the things that are repeatedly said about Washington would have to include the summers, the winters, the traffic, the nightlife, and the ambience.

Complaints about the weather fall into two rather unremarkable categories: heat and humidity in summer, cold and snow in winter. A look at the record book will show that the District, in fact, does not excel in either of the measurable aspects of summer mugginess, but on a sweltering August day, it's not much consolation to know that it's even worse in Houston, Biloxi, and Terre Haute. The snow is something else again. Washington winters are statistically mild — enough so that snow-removal equipment has never been an item in the District's budget. However, when it gets around to snowing, it snows a lot: 19 inches in one blizzard in 1979, for instance. At times like that, Washington slips and slides to a standstill.

Washington traffic is legendary, and no story of the city is complete without some mention of the Lincoln Memorial Circle. It is true that L'Enfant's grand design did not take the automobile into account, since the design — and the city — are older than the automobile by some 150 years.

The trick, of course, is to know where and how you're going, but even then the pace and aggressiveness of the drivers may come as a surprise.

Comments about the nightlife have one main thrust: there isn't any. This, of course, is hard to gauge: Washington appears, at least, to have enough bars, discos and nightclubs, theater and cultural events, to accommodate the people who enjoy them. The District resident, in fact, may be inclined to think there's too much nightlife, rather than too little, but he'd be taking into account the enormous volume of official entertaining that takes place behind closed doors in the foreign embassies and private homes of officials at all levels.

It has also been said of Washington that it lacks the instantly recognizable character of a New York, San Francisco, or New Orleans. That is true, but the reason Washington isn't much like any of those places is because it's so much like itself. Anyone who has lived and worked in the capital is likely to agree that there is an unmistakable feel about the place. In some undefinable way, it is like no other city on earth. Part of it is the charm of a city where history may count for more than it does elsewhere. And some of it is the excitement that is inescapable at the seat of the world's most powerful government. But underlying the excitement and the charm is a mysterious local atmosphere of tentativeness, a sense of impermanence. This may go far back in the city's history, to an era when a shift in administration meant, in effect, a shift in population because all jobs were political. Even today, the Washingtonian is likely not to be a native.

There may never have been a time since its founding that Washington has been free of talk about moving the Federal Government elsewhere. It reached a kind of crescendo after the Civil War, when it was seriously proposed in Congress that the capital be relocated in the Mississippi Valley. Throughout the 1950s the most unquenchable rumor in a rumor-ridden city was that the Government would be moved to Denver "to guard against atomic attack and economize on air conditioning." But lately it seems there has been an unconscious decision to forget about moving elsewhere and settle in on the banks of the Potomac forever. It's about time, too, because neither the Government nor anyone else is likely to find a prettier or more pleasant place to do business.

— W.C.

School-Trip Washington

In the years immediately following World War II, one of the Washington papers could be counted on to run a late-winter news-story with a headline like: "Capital Braces. Estimate Two Million Visitors." Maybe the figure was only one million; whatever it was, at the time it seemed like a great many. Today the capital handles more than 20-million-plus a year and the figure is still rising. Buried among these millions is that loyal core of springtime high school excursionists, college students, and the American families — the bulk of the visitors — and an increasing number of foreign visitors. It's a good bet that virtually the entire 20-plus million will return home even more enthusiastic than when they came. The reason is obvious. Washington is just about the most broadly enjoyable destination in the history of travel.

For anyone who is intellectually curious, the capital can be endlessly fascinating. In the two-and-a-half miles separating the Folger Shakespeare Library on Capitol Hill from the Kennedy Center for the Performing Arts, overlooking the Potomac, there may be more engrossing sights and activities than in any comparable stretch in the world. Even if the curious visitor didn't read a single book from the 11 million at the Library of Congress, his lifetime might be consumed trying to have a look at the 60-to-70-million items in the custody of the Smithsonian Institution, or the 100-thousand art objects at the National Gallery, or rummaging in the millions of records in the National Archives. Fatigue, or old age, would set in long before he got to the top of the Washington Monument, toured the White House, saw the population "clock" at the Department of Commerce, or heard a concert at the Kennedy Center.

The best advice to the visitor is to stroll around a bit and see the city from the outside before plunging into its museums, galleries, and public buildings. In fact, a walk down The Mall from the Capitol to the Lincoln

Memorial is probably a good prescription for cooling the senses and getting accustomed to the scale of the place. The broad marble steps of John Russell Pope's National Gallery, or the edge of the Reflecting Pool, or the steps of the Lincoln Memorial, itself, invite resting and contemplation. A return route up the south side of The Mall will take the stroller past its oldest completed structure, the red sandstone "castle" of the Smithsonian. Back on Capitol Hill — simply "the Hill" in Washington talk — the visitor is sure to have a deepened appreciation of L'Enfant's "noble prospect" as he looks westward over The Mall toward the Virginia Hills.

Before the air age, most visitors were introduced to the nation's capital as they stepped from the darkness of the lovably cavernous old Union Station into the Plaza. Few thrills can match that first sudden sight of the great white dome of the Capitol looming above the trees, the noise of the cars and taxis around the Columbus Monument Circle. The visitor finds himself at the hub of the nation's business. A five minute walk would see him shaking hands with one of his Senators at the Senate Office Building just across the Plaza; another five and he could be standing in the Capitol rotunda.

With a multi-million dollar face lift, the old Union Station has been converted into the National Visitor Center. A sleek new Union Station has been built just yards behind it. The visitor has merely to detrain and walk through the Visitor Center to the Plaza.

In Washington, all things seem to relate to the Capitol. Streets radiate from it, dividing the city into quadrants. Even taxi fare zones are measured from the Hill.

The original design for the Capitol came from an amateur architect, William Thornton. The building was constructed in fits and starts, burned by the British in 1814, and not really finished until 1863, when T. U. Walter's 16-million pound cast-iron dome was raised over the original. Maybe we dare not think of the Capitol as finished yet. In the 1950s Congress ordered the East Front enlarged and refaced with marble, and some members are beginning to eye the West Front. Inside the Capitol there is a lot for the visitor to see — House and Senate chambers, committee meetings, statuary, murals, inscriptions, and the senate subway.

The visitor may welcome the brisk walk across the East Capitol Plaza to reach the severely classical, white marble front of the Supreme

Court Building. The Court has occupied part of the Capitol through most of its history, and when it got its own building in the 1930s, it seemed natural that it would be on the Hill. Inside, architect Cass Gilbert's building is rich in marble, heavy wood paneling, thick carpeting, and velour trappings. The solemn, muffled atmosphere makes plain that some weighty thinking goes on behind those heavy doors. The great spiral staircase is a surprise feature and its elliptical curves help soften somewhat the building's angular severity.

Immediately south of the Court building is the green-domed Library of Congress, whose priceless contents make up for its Renaissance architecture. In contrast the studied absence of decoration from the attractive Annex — appropriately named for Thomas Jefferson — helps strike a startling balance between the two as they face each other across 2nd Street S.E. Congress' own library has grown into the world's largest and it has custody of over a 100-million items — housed in numerous buildings — with no end in sight. The new Madison Building, south of the Capitol, will help ease the pressure for space. All this grew from Jefferson's personal library — 6,000 volumes — which he sold to Congress after its collection had burned.

In a city of libraries the Library of Congress is breathtaking in its comprehensiveness. Its reference service — established for the convenience of Congress, but available to all — has no equal. Within the building the rococo marble staircase and the central reading room are indoor landmarks. The "Library" is not all books. Its Coolidge Auditorium presents some of the best classical music in town.

No person of literary interests should leave the Hill without taking in the Folger Shakespeare Library. Although the library is administered by Amherst College, benefactor Henry Clay Folger wisely directed that it be built in the highly accessible national capital. In addition to housing one of the world's greatest collections of English literature and Shakespeareana, the Folger has a usable replica of an early 17th-century London theater and exhibits of Elizabethan life and customs.

As the visitor descends from Capitol Hill to The Mall, the first attraction he will encounter is the U.S. Grant Memorial. Among the District's statuary, the Grant Memorial is the biggest, with lots of bronze Union troopers and snorting horses attending the Commanding General

(Grant was the Army's finest horseman). One of the best of the many equestrian statues that decorate Washington's traffic circles is Gutzon Borglum's fighting Phil Sheridan. Among the most moving (and non-equestrian) is Felix deWeldon's Marine Corps Memorial in Arlington. The recent trend in memorials is toward abstraction like the Robert Taft Memorial.

Dominating the east end of The Mall is the white marble expanse of the National Gallery of Art, flanked by its brand new, triumphantly modern East Wing. Sometimes still called the Mellon Gallery after its first benefactor, Andrew Mellon, the National has grown into one of the world's most important art museums. Traditionally, its immense collection has run toward old masters and Europeans. This policy is rapidly changing, especially with the advent of the East Wing, which features a giant Calder mobile and some spectacular contemporary outdoor sculpture.

Before he does anything else, any American leaving the National Gallery by the front should dash across Constitution Avenue to the National Archives. There, after passing through the world's largest bronze doors, he can see with his own eyes three of history's most important documents, the Declaration of Independence, the Constitution, and the Bill of Rights. Elsewhere in the building there are enough documents, microfilm, and curios to satisfy 200 years of snooping. But these three are the most significant.

It's hard to define the Smithsonian Institution. Known affectionately as "the nation's attic," it is part museum, part archive, part art gallery, part publishing house, part science lab, part zoo, part theater, part concert hall, and much more. The Smithsonian has varying degrees of administrative responsibility for such diverse public charges as the National Gallery, the National Zoo, the Canal Zone Biological Area, and the Kennedy Center. Crowning the paradox, it is a private foundation, charged by the government with these many tasks and given appropriations as necessary. Founder James Smithson, illegimate son of an English peer, suffered much neglect in his lifetime. He left half-a-million dollars to a classless country he had never visited to found a society for the "increase of knowledge." If Smithson sought immortality, he hit the jackpot. The organization he helped found now outdraws even Disneyland. In 1904 the Englishman's body was brought to the U.S. for reburial in downtown

Washington. For most visitors the red stone headquarters building, which looks like the set for a film version of Scott's *Ivanhoe*, the Natural History, and History and Technology Museums, and the National Air and Space Museum are the heart and soul of the Smithsonian and The Mall.

Esthetically, the Washington Monument may be the most satisfying structure in the capital. There is a kind of magic in the way its clean, vertical lines hover over a markedly horizontal city. At 555 feet, 5 and 1/8 inches, the most visible landmark in the capital area, the Monument is the tallest masonry structure in the world, likely never to be topped in this age of steel-girded structures. It has nothing to fear locally from skyscrapers, because the Fine Arts Commission limits the height of buildings in downtown Washington. At one time a favorite visitor's ritual was to climb the 898 steps to the top, but this is no longer permitted. Today, everyone must take the elevator and content themselves with the challenge of reading 189 dedicatory inscriptions as they walk down.

From the Monument the obvious place to head next is the Lincoln Memorial, located at the other end of the Reflecting Pool. The building is remarkably compact for its size, and its balance of horizontal and vertical lines complement perfectly the powerful upward thrust of the Monument and the rounded, rambling character of the Capitol, two miles distant. The addition of the Reflecting Pool proved to be a stroke of genius. There is no question, either, about the impact of its interior. The chamber containing Daniel Chester French's giant statue of a brooding Lincoln has become one of the unofficial sanctuaries of the nation.

When the Kennedy Center for the Performing Arts opened in 1971, its opera house, concert hall, and theater instantly added a new dimension to cultural life in the capital. The world's leading artists vie to play the Kennedy Center. The Center is the vision of the distinguished American architect, Edward Durell Stone. Its Grand Foyer, more than 600 feet long, is dominated by Robert Berks' controversial giant bust of the late President, and has become one of the most popular meeting places of Washington's society.

With thousands of visitors a day lined up hoping to get in, the White House must be the best known residence in the country. It became white after British incendiaries had scorched the sandstone exterior in 1814 and Congress decided it would be cheaper to paint it than to make repairs. It was not until the administration of Teddy Roosevelt almost a century later that the new title appeared on official Presidential stationery. More than the most familiar residence, the White House may be the most renovated in the country. Each President has the prerogative of decorating the house as he sees fit. In Truman's administration the insides of the building were scooped out and reconstructed, perhaps the most prodigious residential remodeling in history. The history and decor of the East Room, the Blue Room, the Oval Office, the State Dining room, and the Lincoln Bedroom are a familiar part of the national lore.

Historic Lafayette Square across Pennsylvania Avenue from the White House was intended by L'Enfant to be the President's front yard. In proper republican fashion, George Washington scotched the idea of so much real estate being assigned to the Chief Executive, and ordered it made a public park. Through much of the city's history, the Square was its most fashionable address. Today the Square is largely institutionalized and only Decatur House and the Dolley Madison House remain of the many historic mansions that once lined the park. St. John's Episcopal Church, "the church of the Presidents," actually faces 16th Street, but is counted in the ambience of the square. No one is quite sure why Andrew Jackson's statue holds the center of a park named for Lafayette, while the Marquis' statue is thrust into the southeast corner. It is best seen in late spring, when the magnolias are in bloom.

No architecture buff should miss the Old Executive Office Building just west of the White House. Built in Grant's administration to house the Departments of State, War, and Navy, it is a masterpiece of late Victorian ebullience, featuring columns upon columns, dormers, chimneys, and assorted decorated gimcracks to delight the eye. Inside it is a labyrinth of tiled hallways, lined in dark wood, which lead to an abundance of high-ceilinged, dark and comfortable looking offices. Directly across Pennsylvania Avenue from "Old State" is Blair-Lee House, the nation's official guest home. Understandably, neither is open to the public.

The "Stars and Stripes" at Washington Monument

The Capitol Building

Washington Monument reflected in the Tidal Basin

Lincoln Memorial

Abraham Lincoln statue, Lincoln Memorial

Thomas Jefferson statue, Jefferson Memorial

Jefferson Memorial

The White House, from Lafayette Square

Vietnam Memorial

Iwo Jima Memorial

Botanic Gardens

The White House, from the south lawn

Washington Monument

"Old Glory" and the Capitol Building

Library of Congress

John F. Kennedy Memorial for the Performing Arts

Botanic Gardens

Smithsonian Institution

Washington Cathedral

Supreme Court Building

Lincoln Memorial

Andrew Jackson statue, Lafayette Square

Washington Monument

The Capitol Building and The Mall

Arts and Industries Building, Smithsonian Institution

Health and Human Services Building

Lincoln Memorial

The Capitol Building

National Visitors Center

The Treasury Building

Shrine of the Immaculate Conception

Jefferson Memorial

Lincoln Memorial from Washington Monument

Memorial Amphitheater, Arlington National Cemetery

Georgetown University

Tomb of the Unknown Soldier, Arlington National Cemetery

Tomb of the Unknown Soldier, Arlington National Cemetery

"Changing of the Guard," Tomb of the Unknown Soldier

National Air and Space Museum

National Museum of American History

The Capitol Building

Rayburn House Office Building

President John F. Kennedy grave, Arlington National Cemetery

Church of Jesus Christ of Latter Day Saints Temple

Vietnam Memorial statue

The Watergate Complex

Howard University Library

Mt. Vernon, Virginia, historic home of George Washington

The Work-a-day Capital

On any Monday morning, while the sightseer is still yawning in his motel room, federal workers, civilian and military, are headed for their offices. They leave from red-brick rowhouses around Lincoln Park, estates in Potomac, garden apartments in Arlington, "dormitories" near DuPont Circle, stucco cottages in Takoma Park, ramblers in Silver Spring, and high-rises in Rosslyn. By the tens of thousands they stream into the Federal Triangle, the venerable, many winged Interior Department, the Department of Labor fortress near the Capitol, Foggy Bottom's State Department headquarters, the beautifully-housed Department of Housing and Urban Development in L'Enfant Plaza, and many more.

Additional thousands travel away from the city toward the out-of-town sites favored by low-profile officialdom — to the stolid whiteness of CIA headquarters in Langley, Virginia, the glassy expanse of the NSA operations building at Fort Meade, Maryland, or the Atomic Energy Commission at Germantown, Maryland. The servants of the Republic travel mostly by private car and bus but increasingly by the sleek new Metrorail system, which links points as distant as Laurel, Maryland, and Dulles International Airport. By the time the visitor is ready to tackle the curving exhibit halls of the Hirshhorn Museum, Uncle Sam's business is in high gear.

The legendary Pentagon Building, the Defense Department's headquarters in Arlington, is hardly typical of federal workspace. This is all the more reason for taking a closer look. It's convenient too; just eight minutes by Metro's Blue Line from Metro Center. The parking lot holds an impressive 8,000 cars, but the Defense Department admits to having more than 22,000 workers reporting every day. Some observers think that it may be as high as 30,000, which would match the population of

Maryland's capital, Annapolis. The Pentagon was begun four months before Pearl Harbor and completed by January of 1943. The 83-million-dollar price tag may have seemed outrageously high then, but the building probably could not be duplicated today for ten to 15 times that amount and certainly not in that length of time. It was not a bad price for what was to be for a quarter-century the world's largest office building. Depending upon whether you view New York's World Trade Center as one building or a complex, the Pentagon may *still* be the world's largest office building. Anyway, with its 6,546,360-square feet of workspace, there can be no doubt that it is the world's largest five-story office building.

Even 36 years after its construction, the Pentagon's figures are still startling. Its 17-1/2 miles of corridors provide its occupants access to 685 drinking fountains, 285 washrooms, 10 snack bars, and six cafeterias. The famous Concourse with its bank, post office, department store, and miscellaneous shops might do service as a shopping mall in a small town. The building has no elevators and each section of its outer ring is 921 feet long. A lunchtime jog around the building would cover just about a mile.

Architect G.E. Bergstrom's unusual design has proved not only functional and durable, but a bit mysterious as well. The five-story building has five concentric five-side rings, connected by ten radial corridors and surrounding a central court that measures exactly five acres. All this has raised speculation about its symbolism — the wagon train in a circle, for instance — but no one has come up with a totally convincing interpretation. In figurative language the case has been quite different. Since the business of its tenants is of some concern to people of the world who speak a hundred or so different languages, "pentagon" may be the world's most widely and immediately understood metaphor. The building's undramatic configuration has worn well with most observers over the years, and it may be that the Pentagon, along with the Washington Monument, will survive changes in taste better than most other structures in Washington.

The frequent references to Washington as "a one-industry city" or a "company town" can mislead the visitor about the true nature of the population. There's no denying that having 500,000-plus residents on a single payroll can create a tilt in the local economy. The real surprise in this figure, however, is that it represents only about one-fourth of the capital area's work force. Contrary to popular notion, not everyone in

Washington works for the Federal Government, not even indirectly. It stands to reason that Government workers need to be housed, clothed, fed, transported, made secure, lobbied, entertained, spied on, and cured of affliction, both physical and spiritual. This calls for a lot of non-Federal help. We may speculate, then, that for each Government stenographer, there is a hairdresser, a bank clerk, and a cocktail waitress; for each official in a regulatory agency, three lawyers in private practice. There are over 1,200,000 other wage earners in the metropolitan area whose work brings them only infrequently into direct contact with the activities of government.

In a curious way, a bit in the spirit of a medieval city, some of Washington's major streets attract to themselves particular activities. Massachusetts Avenue has long been "embassy row." Pennsylvania Avenue has always been very much a Federal boulevard, route of Presidents and victorian armies. Connecticut is a business street — banks, offices, hotels, restaurants — in the spirit of the U.S. Chamber of Commerce, which stands at its foot. Sixteenth Street is the avenue of the national associations and, secondarily, an embassy row. Whatever L'Enfant's wishes were in the matter, the original naming of streets did not foresee a great growth. Numbering the north-south streets is an old American custom, handy because you can't conveniently run out of numbers, but lettering the east-west streets was another matter. Just as soon as the city had grown north 26 blocks, there was a problem. This was resolved for the moment by beginning a new alphabet of two-syllable names — Adams, Belmont, Chapin, etc. Progress pushed the city engineers through Upshur, Varnum, and Webster faster than anticipated and letter carriers found themselves working a third alphabet of three syllable names — Allison, Buchanan, Crittenden. A fourth alphabet was inevitable. This one took horticultural names and mercifully the District line ended the emergency at Verbena Street.

Through its first hundred years, Washington scarcely rated a foreign embassy and not many delegations either. That's because it wasn't considered a very important capital. All that has changed. At a recent count, there were 128 of them, most clustered along Massachusetts Avenue N.W. between DuPont Circle and the Naval Observatory. It isn't clear why Massachusetts Avenue attracted so many foreign missions, but it must have something to do with the availability of mansions and town-houses suitable to be converted to chancelleries. The large and attractive British Embassy, just below the Naval Observatory, has long ranked as one of the showcases of embassy row, The clean design of the Venezuelan Embassy at 24th Street also draws favorable comment.

Washington has on occasion been described as a city of churches. Since there are only about 500 churches, this must refer to their architectural splendor. Washington Cathedral, the biggest, dominates the skyline of northwest Washington, partly because of its size, partly because it is on one of the highest spots in the city. The National Shrine of the Immaculate Conception, near Catholic University, comes off almost as well in elevation. Looming above the thick trees in the residential northern half of the city, the two cathedrals offer a nice balance to the skyline of public buildings in downtown Washington. The sixth largest church in the world, Washington Cathedral is nominally Episcopalian, but is open for use by all worshippers. In design it is the traditional Gothic, but there has been an effort in recent years to incorporate into it the work of modern artists and artisans. It fits attractively into the popular cathedral close, one of Washington's favorite gardens, and has the admirable feature of being all masonry.

Among the most interesting and attractive ecclesiastical buildings in the city is the Washington Mosque on Massachusetts Avenue above Sheridan Circle. The limestone shrine is the center of Islamic worship in Washington and is shared by members of the many foreign missions from Moslem nations.

Georgetown

Georgetown may be America's most fashionable address. Actually, the U.S. Postal Service won't let you use Georgetown in the address, at least not since 1895, when the town officially became part of Washington D.C. However, if you can't have Georgetown *for* an address, you can still manage a Georgetown address. Of course you may have to content yourself with a prosaic legend like 2715 Q Street N.W., Washington D.C. 20007. But this shouldn't cause worry. Any Washington hostess who knows her P and Q streets will recognize instantly that it falls within the enchanted enclave. Prosaic or not, anyone should be more than content with that address. It's that of the elegant Dumbarton House, maintained as an historic shrine by the Colonial Dames.

Georgetown was first settled in the 17th century as a thriving river port town, and was chartered by the Crown, all before Pierre L'Enfant was even born. To the chagrin of a few socially sensitive Georgetowners, however, it was discovered not long ago that the town was not named for one of the Hanoverian kings but for a Scottish indentured servant, who was the area's first squatter. George Washington, who lived just ten or 15 miles down river, frequented the little town throughout his life. It was at Suter's Tavern, somewhere near present-day K Street N.W., that he called the first meeting of commissioners to discuss plans for the new federal capital.

If Georgetown is just a part of Washington now, asks the visitor, how can I tell when I'm there? Well, if you find yourself walking for a succession of blocks over quaint but sometimes uneven brick sidewalks, through quiet streets where elms sometimes arch the roadway, past dozens and dozens of handsome federal-style, Victorian and modern townhouses, most sporting polished brass door knockers, you are probably in Georgetown. If on a teeming commercial street, it suddenly strikes you that art galleries outnumber the fast-food restaurants, you know for sure that you are in Georgetown. If you are one who craves a more concrete orientation, know that as you cross Rock Creek Parkway traveling west on M Street N.W., you are in Georgetown the instant your front bumper reaches the intersection with Pennsylvania Avenue.

After all he has read in the guide books about stately Georgetown, the visitor might be disconcerted by the strong commercial character of M Street. He will discover to his relief that almost all business in Georgetown is confined to this street and to Wisconsin Avenue. Right in the midst of the crush of boutiques, restaurants, and nightclubs is the oldest surviving house in the Washington area, the Old Stone House, built in 1766. It is maintained by the Park Service and is open to the public as a museum of colonial life in the area. At the east end of the same block is a fine old 18th-century structure, the Thomas Sim Lee Corner, the first Georgetown building saved from the wrecker's ball under the provisions of the Old Georgetown Act.

This act of Congress is intended to help preserve historically or architecturally important buildings within Georgetown. It also restored a measure of the former town's identity. For example, Georgetowners were permitted to raise street signs that added old street names — Needwood, Wapping, Gay, East Lane, Cherry Alley, et. al. — to those imposed by the Post Office. The story of Francis Scott Key Bridge, which links Georgetown to Arlington, Virginia, is a parable illustrating why the Old Georgetown Act is necessary. In the 1920s Congress authorized construction of the graceful span to succeed the old aqueduct Bridge and honor the memory of Georgetown's most famous native son. The building contractors promptly tore down the house that Key had been born in to make way for the approaches to the new bridge.

From M Street the visitor is well advised to divert a block south to see the old C.&O. Canal before tackling the main part of Georgetown. The historic canal, which floated its last payload in 1924, runs the length of Georgetown parallel to the K Street Viaduct and continues all the way to Cumberland, Maryland. Large stretches of the canal are maintained by the National Park Service, and in summer, mule-powered barge trips are conducted by Park Service personnel from Georgetown to Brookmont, Maryland. George Washington was one of the early boosters and stockholders in the Canal Company, but it didn't open until the late 1820s and by the time the appearance of the railroads reduced it to relative unimportance. As a tourist attraction in the last 60 years, the old canal has probably returned its construction cost several times over. The canal towpath is one of the capital's most popular hiking routes, and in the Georgetown stretch, the tiny, colorful houses that line the canal — called with disarming logic, the Towpath Houses — may be the choicest of all residences for young Washington singles. On 31st Street, close to the Canal, is fashionable Canal Square, a complex of shops and restaurants housed in a converted warehouse.

Any stranger turning without warning into Wisconsin Avenue on a Saturday morning may be excused for supposing that he has stumbled on an oriental bazaar, a riot, or both. Sidewalk vendors peddle an infinite variety of merchandise and reduce walking space to a minimum. Hordes of shoppers from all corners of the capital area crowd into gourmet shops, boutiques, record shops, cafés, and art galleries that were in many instances designed to accommodate no more than a dozen persons. In addition to generating revenue, the Saturday morning scene has environmental advantages. The crowd makes Wisconsin Avenue virtually impassable to auto traffic and thereby improves the local air quality. The Saturday morning tradition may have begun innocently back in the 1950s, when the wives of rising young government officials liked to soak up some of the Georgetown glamor by walking the quiet, well-tended streets and browsing in its few and decorous shops.

Georgetown has between 40 and 50 houses of historic distinction and not all are row houses or townhouses. A few are mansions on small estates. Tudor Place on 31st Street is one of the larger dwellings, and by consensus one of Georgetown's most attractive. "Tudor" is a misnomer: the house is a distinguished representative of Federal design in yellow stucco. It was created by Dr. William Thornton, designer of the Capitol, and built for a granddaughter of Martha Washington. It has been occupied by the same family for seven generations. Another of the larger Georgetown showcases is Evermay, a superb Georgian manor house with lovely formal grounds, which stands at the head of 28th Street. Looking at its lush and quiet garden, it is hard to believe that the bumper-to-bumper traffic of Massachusetts Avenue is less than a mile east, just beyond Rock Creek Parkway.

Even Washingtonians sometimes get confused about the difference between Dumbarton House and Dumbarton Oaks. Dumbarton House is the genteel late-Georgian house on Q Street, and could claim to be the oldest house in Georgetown. Dumbarton Oaks is a small urban estate lying north of R Street and west of Oak Hill Cemetery. It may lie outside the boundaries established by the Old Georgetown Act, but no matter. It fits in beautifully with everything else. The 19th-century mansion is now a museum of Byzantine and Roman art and is administered by Harvard University. It was the scene of the first meeting held to discuss the formation of the United Nations, and so may qualify as the birthplace of that organization. The eastern edge of the property is bordered by a charming flowered walkway, known unofficially as Lovers' Lane.

Georgetown has the singular good fortune to be bounded by belts of green on almost every side, on the east by Rock Creek Parkway, on the South by the C.&O. Canal, on the north by Oak Hill Cemetery, and on the west by the largest swatch, the campus of Georgetown University. Founded by Maryland's Archbishop Carroll in the 1780s, Georgetown University is the oldest Roman Catholic college in America. Among its many attractive buildings, Old North goes back to within a year or two of the founding of the University.

Georgetown can be both a joy and a frustration to the visitor. While its charming streets may have the air of a museum, may even conjure up recollections of historic restorations like Williamsburg and Sturbridge Village, the fact is that whole families daily live, work, and play behind almost every one of those polished door knockers. Unless you happen to know a resident or two, there is no way you can discover what those glamorous houses look like inside. There's one exception. Sometime in the spring, a number of Georgetowners open their houses and gardens for annual tours. If you are lucky, enterprising, or downright aggressive, you might obtain a ticket. It's worth the effort. Gardens, incidentally, are another thing secluded behind most of the handsome facades, an estimated 4,000 of them, some very tiny. The garden at Dumbarton Oaks, open to the public most of the year, is probably the biggest by far.

The Green Hills

No major city in America is more fortunate than Washington in the beauty, variety, and generally unspoiled character of its environs — near and far. It is a remarkable turn of events when one considers that this Upper Potomac River location was agreed upon not for reasons of its natural endowments, but on grounds of geography and then purely as a matter of political expediency. In 1790 Thomas Jefferson entertained Alexander Hamilton at a gentlemanly dinner in New York and the two came to a gentleman's agreement. Jefferson would support Hamilton's important money bill in Congress and Hamilton would use his influence to locate the new federal capital outside the teeming Northeast. The compromise pointed inevitably to a site on the Potomac, which lay just about halfway between Boston and Charleston.

Washington lies midway between the Appalachian foothills on the west and the Chesapeake Bay wetlands on the east. In this part of the country there can be a remarkable variation in terrain even within a short distance. Although downtown Washington is flat and marshy, the terrain rises rapidly in all directions, from about sea level at the Zero Milestone on the Ellipse to over 400 feet at the beginning of the third alphabet on Connecticut Avenue, less than four miles away. Except to the northeast, where the land gradually flattens into the sandy, piny estuary country, the countryside around the capital is one of low, rolling hills, noticeably free of the landmarks of heavy industry that have become the heritage of so many cities.

One of the best spots from which to gain an appreciation of Washington's favored situation is less than a mile from the Lincoln Memorial — Arlington National Cemetery. Two of the most moving prospects at Arlington are from the porch of the Custis-Lee Mansion, now officially called Arlington House, and the Tomb of the Unknown Soldier. Looking across the river toward the capital from even this short distance affords an impression of a clean and spacious city encircled by pleasant green hills. Arlington National Cemetery, in fact, may be the very best place for any visitor to begin a look around at Washington's environs. The most famous American military cemetery, Arlington contains the graves of many national heroes as well as the graves of approximately 200,000 veterans of the Armed Forces. The two most often visited in the park are those of the Unknown Soldier and the late President John F. Kennedy. Veterans as diverse in fame as Earl Warren, William Jennings Bryan, Phil Sheridan, Pierre L'Enfant, and John Foster Dulles are also buried here.

The presence of the attractive Custis-Lee Mansion in the cemetery is anomalous and a reminder that it became a military cemetery by chance. Once the home of Robert E. Lee, the mansion was seized early in the Civil War by the Union Army, who used it for a headquarters building. With the arrival of so many dead from many battles in nearby Northern Virginia, the Army began to bury them on the slopes below the mansion. After the war Lee never got his property back, although the Federal Government made a cash settlement with the Lee family. And so the advent of a national cemetery.

No one should leave Arlington without seeing the Iwo Jima Monument in the northern corner just off Arlington Boulevard. Sculptor Felix deWeldon's massive bronze group was movingly modeled after Joe Rosenthal's famous news photo taken atop Mount Suribachi and is usually identified instantly by young and old alike. It's the largest statue in the capital and is appropriately placed close to one of the area's busiest roadways.

Fifteen miles downriver from Arlington is Mount Vernon, the comely estate of a man who knew well, and deeply appreciated, the charms of the local countryside. No matter the cost in time and money, every American should make the pilgrimage to the restored home of George Washington. The place speaks volumes about the kind of men who made the American Revolution. No romantic, intellectual revolutionaries these. The master of Mount Vernon and his colleagues from north and south alike were prosperous men, energetic men, optimistic men. In the Age of Reason, they never hesitated to apply it, but they applied it largely to getting things done, and with luck, turning a profit. Listen to the guide tell about Mount Vernon's 8,000 acres of tobacco, cereal grains and other crops, of the hundreds of head of livestock, the gardens, the craft shops, and the hundreds of workers, most of whom had to be fed right on the plantation. Handling the Presidency must have seemed easier by comparison. About 150 years before Calvin Coolidge, in Vermont candor, articulated the national credo, George Washington must have understood that "the business of America is business."

One of the most pleasant discoveries in all the Washington area is that Mount Vernon can be reached by river boat, which leaves from Southwest Washington's Water Street and makes the four-hour excursion twice a day. The unhurried cruise down the wide river can add a nice touch of nostalgia to the visit. But those who drive down the George Washington Memorial Parkway can take comfort in their greater flexibility of schedule. They have time to visit Alexandria's charming Old Town and grab a Virginia ham sandwich from the hand of a costumed waitress at the restored colonial Gadsby's Tavern. They can even stop off at the George Washington National Masonic Memorial, in design, one of the most curious buildings in the capital area. The view of Washington from the Memorial may be even better than the one from Arlington.

Mount Vernon, now reduced to 500 acres, has been preserved, restored, and is lovingly maintained by the Mount Vernon Ladies Association. In the 1850s over much hard-headed 19th-century resistance, they saved the estate from being turned into a hotel and probably eventually demolished. Not a nickel of tax money went into its salvation. The ladies raised it all privately. To get the proper feel of the place, the visitor should allow not less than half a day for wandering, snooping, reflecting. Even at its present 500 acres, it is extremely impressive with its tree-lined avenues, extensive formal gardens, its dozen or more outbuildings, well-manicured grounds and, of course, the mansion house itself. Seen from close up, the wooden mansion may not appear quite so regal as it does on picture postcards, but it could still hold its own today in a fashionable suburb of a large city. Despite the greater durability (and dampness) of their stone manor houses, few Englishmen of Washington's day could have lived in more baronial splendor than this. Washington was lord and master over more than 200 black slaves and dozens of white laborers and artisans, who produced almost everything needed for life right on his own place.

On the Maryland side of the Potomac, the most attractive route into the back country is by consensus the C.&O. Canal Towpath. Hiking along the towpath may come close to being the single most popular outdoor activity among Washingtonians. The picturesque path, beautifully graded by the pounding of mule-hoofs over a century of time, is now part of a Historic National Park that extends from the Canal's tidewater terminus in Georgetown to Cumberland, Maryland, 185 miles away in the mountains of western Maryland. It's possible to hike the full distance, taking advantage of Park Service campsites along the way, but most Washingtonians content themselves with the stretch between Georgetown and Seneca, Maryland. Some of the locks and the old lock houses have been restored and help add color to the Canal scene.

Perhaps the outstanding scenic attraction along the Canal's route can be found just seven miles upstream from the District of Columbia line — the Great Falls of the Potomac. Here the river comes crashing through a rocky gorge about a mile long — and drops more than 75 feet. It's hard to believe that this is the same river that one sees at Memorial Bridge in Washington, and clearly it's one of the things that must have stimulated the buiding of the Canal. There are two parks here, a state park on the Virginia side in addition to the National Historic Park. On the Maryland side there are sturdy walkways built out over jagged rocks and white water. Alongside the Canal at this point is Great Falls Tavern, built in 1830 and now converted to a museum and Park Service Information Center. The Tavern once offered accommodations to travelers using the canal boats. An average barge speed of two miles an hour suggests that there once must have been a lot more of these hostelries along the Canal's 185 mile length.

The attractive countryside around the capital was coveted early on for a kind of suburban living associated with the raising and riding of horses. This was true on both the Virginia and Maryland sides of the Potomac. There was a time not many years ago when one might see the "hunt country" estates not far from the center of Washington. However, the rapid increase in population in the metropolitan area and the consequent spread of urban density has consigned this bucolic idyll to areas well beyond the Capital Beltway. However, in places as far out as

Middleburg and Warrenton, Virginia, one can still find the stately white mansions sitting on green hillocks and well-seated squires cantering on quiet dirt pathways.

More representative of suburban living in the future is Reston, Virginia, about six miles east of Dulles International Airport. Reston was designed in the early 1960s as a self-contained small city, planned down to the last detail. It has both high and low density neighborhoods, big and small apartment buildings, townhouses, mansions, parks, churches, medical facilities, stores, theaters, even its own lake.

Any visitor who drives as far as Reston should go the extra few miles to Dulles International Airport to see the extraordinary terminal building. The giant but strikingly graceful structure looks as though it might achieve flight with greater ease than the aircraft sitting on its runways. Another stop worth making in this area is at Wolf Trap Farm Park, for the Performing Arts right off the Dulles access road. Few of the musicians and other artists who appear here in summer can have performed elsewhere in such beautiful natural surroundings. At present the theater building (open at the sides) offers seats to only about 3,000. The remainder of the audience appears well content to listen from the grassy slopes.

Washington, D.C. Photography Credits

James Blank: Pages 19, 20, 23, 25, 27, 33, 34, 35, 36, 38, 39, 41, 43, 44, 47, 49, 51, 52, 54, 58, 59, 64.

Shangle Photographics: Pages 17, 22, 24, 28, 29, 30, 31, 37, 40, 45, 46, 48, 50, 53, 57, 60, 61, 63.

Shangle/Borland Photographics: Pages 18, 21, 26, 32, 42, 55, 56, 63.